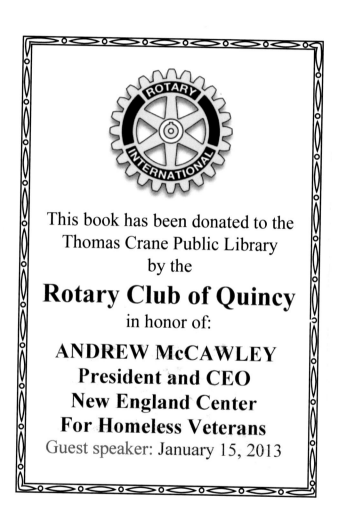

This book has been donated to the
Thomas Crane Public Library
by the

Rotary Club of Quincy
in honor of:

ANDREW McCAWLEY
President and CEO
New England Center
For Homeless Veterans
Guest speaker: January 15, 2013

Science Experiments with Simple Machines

Simple Experiments with
Inclined Planes

Chris Oxlade

WINDMILL
BOOKS
New York

Published in 2014 by Windmill Books, An Imprint of Rosen Publishing
29 East 21st Street, New York, NY 10010

Produced for Windmill by Calcium Creative Ltd
Editors for Calcium Creative Ltd: Sarah Eason and Jennifer Sanderson
Designer: Emma DeBanks

Photo Credits: Cover: Dreamstime: Radzian. Inside: Dreamstime: Ammit 24,
CBpix 28, Dobi 20, Dreamshot 6, Njnightsky 7, Paul Precscott 25, RatManDude
9, Suenos6 5, Tomh1000 15, Vindalv 23; Shutterstock: Auremar 14, Max Blain
8, Vladimir Ivanovich Danilov 17, Juan Ignacio Laboa 29, Timothy Large 27,
Olivier 1, 4, Pryzmat 16, Ronfromyork 12, Javier Rosano 22, Ken Schulze 13,
Artit Thongchuea 26, T.W. van Urk 21; Tudor Photography 10, 11, 18, 19.

Library of Congress Cataloging-in-Publication Data

Oxlade, Chris.
Simple experiments with inclined planes / by Chris Oxlade.
pages cm. — (Science experiments with simple machines)
Includes index.
ISBN 978-1-61533-752-1 (library binding) — ISBN 978-1-61533-821-4 (pbk.) —
ISBN 978-1-61533-822-1 (6-pack)
1. Inclined planes--Experiments—Juvenile literature. 2. Motion—
Experiments—Juvenile literature. I. Title.
TJ147.O884 2014
621.8—dc23
2013003810

Manufactured in the United States of America

CPSIA Compliance Information: Batch #BS13WM: For Further Information contact Windmill Books, New York, New York at 1-866-478-0556

Contents

Simple Machines

What do you think of when you hear the word "machine?" Perhaps you imagine a smartphone, a construction crane, or even an aircraft. Machines are things that make our lives easier, by helping us do jobs. Smartphones, cranes, and aircraft are complicated machines, made up of thousands of parts. However, many machines are very simple. They have only one or two parts. The **inclined plane** is one type of simple machine.

Types of Simple Machines

There are six types of simple machines. Inclined planes are one. The others are **wheel and axles**, **pulleys**, **wedges**, **screws**, and **levers**. You might not guess that they are all machines. Many have no moving parts. However, they still help us do jobs in our everyday lives.

An inclined plane helps lift this heavy container onto a truck.

This inclined plane makes it easy for the builders to roll wheelbarrows up the steps.

What Is an Inclined Plane?

An inclined plane is a ramp or a slope. If you push or roll something up a ramp, walk up a sloping path, or travel up a hill in a car, an inclined plane is helping you. In this book, you will find many examples of inclined planes at work. There are also some interesting experiments for you to do. Try them out and discover for yourself how inclined planes work.

How an Inclined Plane Works

An inclined plane makes lifting heavy objects easier. It makes it easier to move things from one place to another place that is higher. "Inclined" means sloping. A "plane" is a flat surface. An inclined plane is a sloping, flat surface.

Part of an Inclined Plane

An inclined plane is made up of a flat piece of material, the plane. Some inclined planes are made of flat pieces of wood or metal, held up at one end. An example is a wooden ramp that reaches from the ground up to the edge of a dumpster. Ramps must be strong so that they do not bend in the middle. Some inclined planes, such as footpaths, are built on solid, sloping ground.

It is easier to carry a load up a ramp than to lift it straight up.

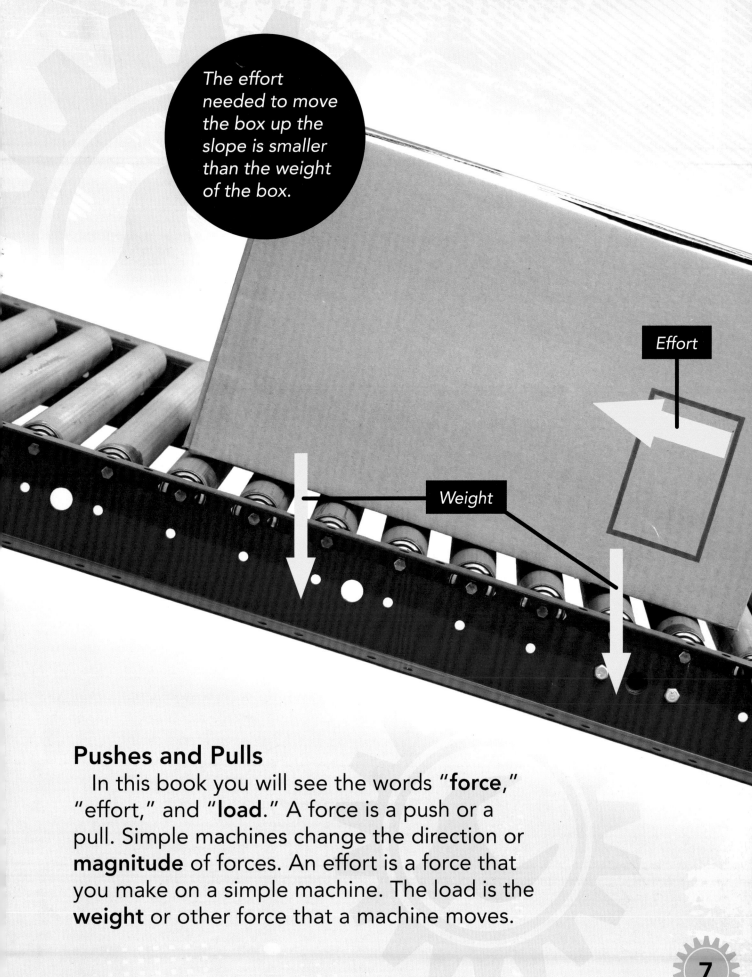

The effort needed to move the box up the slope is smaller than the weight of the box.

Effort

Weight

Pushes and Pulls

In this book you will see the words **"force,"** "effort," and **"load."** A force is a push or a pull. Simple machines change the direction or **magnitude** of forces. An effort is a force that you make on a simple machine. The load is the **weight** or other force that a machine moves.

7

What Is a Ramp?

A ramp is one kind of inclined plane. It is normally a flat piece of material that is held higher at one end than at the other. **Loading ramps** are useful for moving goods on dollies into trucks and other vehicles. It is much easier to use a ramp than to lift heavy objects straight up from the ground. Here are some examples of loading ramps at work.

Simple Loading Ramps

The simplest type of loading ramp is a wide plank of wood. This can be used on a building site or in a backyard to move a loaded wheelbarrow uphill, or up to the edge of a dumpster. Moving trucks often have a strong metal ramp, which the crew walks up and down to carry heavy items into the truck. Horse trailers and stock cars have loading ramps that the animals use to walk into them.

It takes less effort to move an object up a long, gradual ramp than up a short, steep ramp.

Heavy machinery can be driven up a ramp onto a flatbed truck.

Heavyweight Loading Ramps

Bigger, stronger loading ramps are needed to move very heavy loads up into trucks or onto other vehicles. Trucks that carry other vehicles, such as car carrier trailers and tow trucks, have sturdy ramps at the rear. Cargo aircraft have ramps at the rear for moving heavy cargo on board.

Lifting with a Plane

In this experiment you can compare the effort needed to lift a heavy object with and without a ramp. We have used a skateboard, but you could use a heavy toy car instead.

You will Need:

- A 6-foot (2 m) length of string
- A skateboard
- A large plastic container
- A plank of wood

1 Tie one end of the string around one end of your skateboard, at the truck. This is the part of the skateboard to which the wheels are fixed.

2 Lift up the skateboard by the string. Feel how much effort you need to stop the skateboard from falling back down to the ground.

3 Make a ramp by placing the plank on the plastic container. Rest the skateboard on the ramp. The end of the skateboard with the string should point up the ramp. Pull the string along the ramp and hold it to stop the skateboard from rolling down. How much effort did you need this time?

So Simple!

When you lifted the skateboard using the string, you had to support the whole weight of the skateboard. When you put the skateboard on the ramp, the effort you needed to hold the skateboard was less. The ramp worked as a simple machine to increase the effort you made.

Shallow or Steep?

A shallow inclined plane is one that is only slightly sloping, while a steep inclined plane has more of a slope. It is easier to move an object up a shallow slope than a steeper slope because the effort you need is smaller.

Measuring Steepness

The steepness of a slope is called its **grade** or **gradient**. This is how much the slope rises over a certain distance. For example, if a slope rises 1 foot (30 cm) over 2 feet (60 cm) along the ground, the grade is 1 in 2. This is also called a 50 percent grade, because 1 is 50 percent (or half) of 2. A 1 in 4 slope is called a 25 percent grade, because 1 is 25 percent (or a quarter) of 4.

16 %

A traffic sign shows the steepness of the next hill.

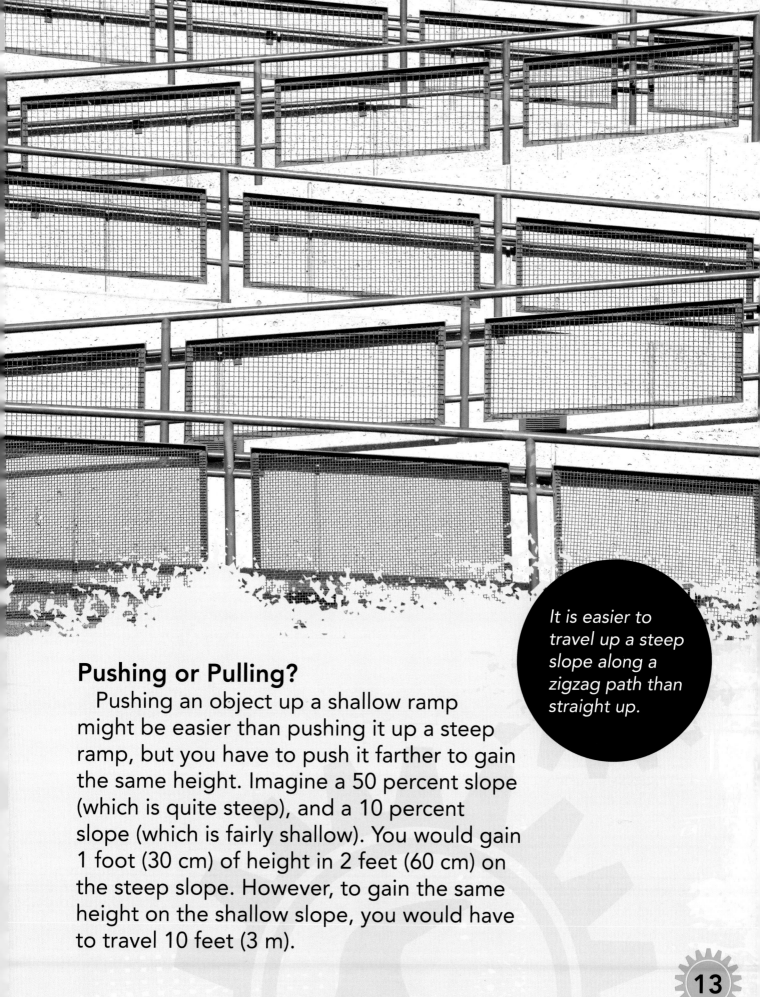

Pushing or Pulling?

Pushing an object up a shallow ramp might be easier than pushing it up a steep ramp, but you have to push it farther to gain the same height. Imagine a 50 percent slope (which is quite steep), and a 10 percent slope (which is fairly shallow). You would gain 1 foot (30 cm) of height in 2 feet (60 cm) on the steep slope. However, to gain the same height on the shallow slope, you would have to travel 10 feet (3 m).

steep and shallow inclined Planes

It may be easier to push or pull something up a shallow slope than a steep slope, but shallow slopes are not always better than steep slopes. Let's take a look at why we use shallow ramps in some places and steep ramps in others.

Shallow Ramps

Gently sloping inclined planes are great for gaining height with just a little effort. We use them where we can make only a small effort on something. A wheelchair ramp is a good example. A person in an wheelchair can push him or herself up a ramp easily without getting tired. Footbridges often have shallow ramps at each end. They make it easy to walk from the sidewalk up to the level of the bridge.

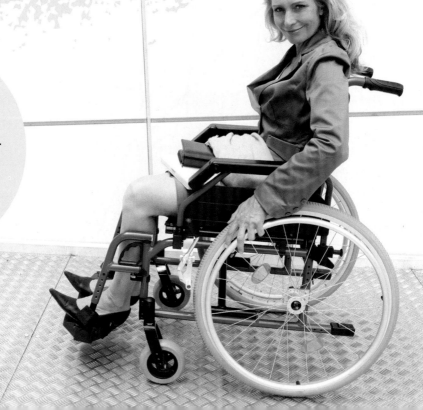

A gently sloping wheelchair ramp makes it easier for wheelchair users to travel uphill.

Steep Ramps

The advantage of a steep ramp is that it gains a lot of height quickly. Moving an object up a steep ramp is still easier than lifting it straight upward. An example is a steep ramp at the start of a roller coaster ride. The ramp allows the cars get to the top of the ride quickly, and the effort needed to pull them up there is less than it would be to lift them up without a ramp.

This steep roller coaster ramp moves the cars quickly to the top.

Going Down

We know now that an inclined plane is a simple machine that helps us to move objects upward. However, it is also useful for moving objects downward. It is easier to lower something down a sloping ramp than to lower it **vertically**.

Slowly Does It

Think about the loading ramps we looked at on page 8. It would be very difficult to lift something heavy straight down from a truck. You would have to support the object's whole weight and bring it slowly down to the ground. Bringing it down an inclined plane would be much easier. You could slide it down, or you could put it on a hand truck and roll it down the inclined plane. You would still need to push or pull to keep the object from sliding too fast or rolling away, but this effort would be less than taking its full weight.

This wheelchair user needs only to pull gently on her wheels to stop herself from moving too fast.

The angle of a skateboard ramp pushes the rider forward as he rolls down.

Wheeling Down

Going down a gently sloping ramp in a wheelchair is easier than going down a steep ramp. It needs only a small effort to stop the wheelchair from rolling away down the slope. It is just the same as riding downhill on your bicycle. You need to brake far less on a shallow slope than on a steep slope.

Steepness and Effort

In this experiment you can investigate how the steepness of an inclined plane affects the amount of effort you need to pull an object up the plane. The stretchiness of the rubber band will show how much force you need.

1 Attach a rubber band to the front of the toy car (you might need some tape for this). Hook the paper clip onto the rubber band.

2 To make a steep inclined plane, prop up one end of the hardcover book with a pile of other books. Put the car at the bottom of the plane and pull it up. Hold the paper clip to stop the car from sliding down. How far does the rubber band stretch?

18

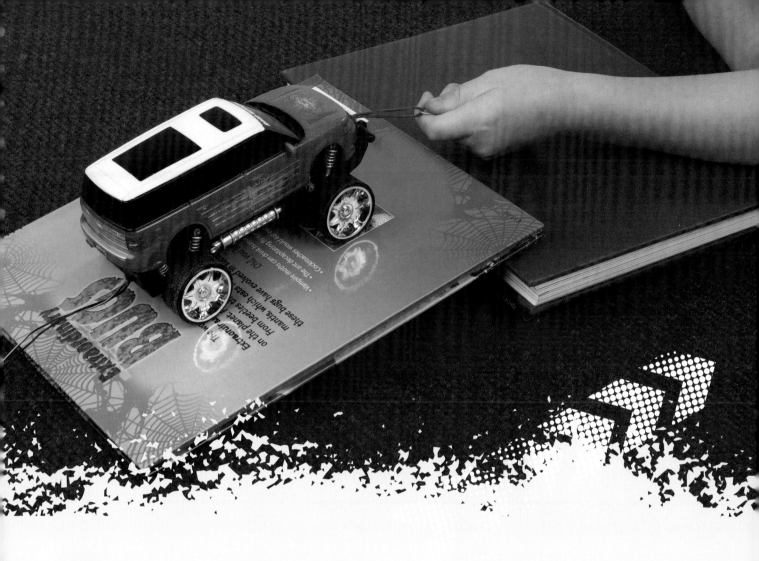

3 Make your inclined plane more shallow by taking some of the books from the pile. Put the car on the plane again and try to pull it up the ramp. Does the rubber band stretch more or less this time?

So Simple!

You should have discovered that the rubber band stretched more on the steep plane than it did on the shallow plane. That is because the shallow plane increased your effort more than the steep plane.

Inclined Planes in the Past

Inclined planes were as important to people in the past as they are today. They were a simple way of moving heavy materials to where they were needed, such as in huge building projects. Inclined planes became even more important after the wheel and axle came into common use.

Pyramids and Planes

Thousands of years ago, the ancient Egyptians built giant stone pyramids. Experts believe that the Egyptians built large, dirt ramps to move enormous blocks of stone up to the level of the pyramids where they were needed. The Egyptians had no other way of lifting the stones. They may have used one very long straight ramp or a ramp that spiraled around the pyramid. The blocks of stone were probably moved up the ramps on wooden rollers.

The giant pyramids at Giza in Egypt were built with the help of inclined planes.

For hundreds of years, inclined planes such as these have been used to haul boats out of the water.

Industrial Planes

In the eighteenth and nineteenth centuries, people often used canals to transport heavy cargo. When they needed to move boats up steep hills, they sometimes built inclined planes to lift boats to higher ground. The trucks were hauled up the slope from the top of the plane. Boats were put in **cradles** and hauled upward along rails.

Inclined Planes and Transportation

An uphill path or road might not look like an inclined plane, but it is one. A gently sloping path is easier to walk up than a steep path, and it is easier for a car to go up a gently sloping hill than a steep hill. Inclined planes also make it safer for vehicles to go downhill.

Sloping Paths

When you walk up a path, you are moving the weight of your body from a lower level to a higher level. The load you are moving is your own weight. The effort is the push you make with your legs to move up the slope. A zigzag path is a gently sloping path that goes back and forth across a hill. Taking the path is much easier than going straight up the hill, although you have to walk much farther.

A zigzag path makes it easier to climb a steep cliff or mountain slope.

A series of gentle slopes linked by sharp bends allows cars to climb steep mountainsides.

Sloping Roads

Gentle slopes allow vehicles to keep traveling at high speeds. On freeways there are always gentle slopes so that cars, trucks, and buses can travel up the hills quickly and easily. In the mountains, roads zigzag up steep hillsides because cars cannot travel straight up.

Trains and Boats

Roads are not the only places that inclined planes are used for transportation. Inclined planes are also found on railroads, at docks, and on canals. They make it easier for trains to move up hills and for ships to be loaded.

Railroad Grades

Trains can go up only very gentle slopes. A slope of 2 percent is about the steepest of grades. Any steeper than that, and a locomotive's wheels would no longer be able to grip the rails. This means that the route of a railroad must be planned very carefully, and bridges and tunnels built to keep the grade as low as possible. In a few places in the world, zigzag railroads are built on steep hills. The trains move back and forth to move up the zigzags.

The zigzags on this railroad line allow trains to climb an almost-vertical hill.

Vehicles are loaded onto a ferry using ramps.

Using Ramps for Ferries

At a ferry dock, vehicles need to drive on and off ferries. There are ramps between the dock and the boat. The ramps tilt up or down and move with the tide as it goes up and down. The ramps allow the vehicles to drive from the dock onto the ferry deck, or from the ferry deck onto the dock.

Zigzags

You need to do some exercise for this last experiment! It is time to test whether zigzag paths make it easier to walk or bike up a steep hill.

1 Start by walking or running straight up the hill. This should feel like really hard work.

2 Go back to the bottom of the hill. This time, go up the hill by taking a zigzag route. Walk across the hill and slightly upward. Change direction every few steps. Is it easier to go up the hill this time?

3 Now, try going up a hill on your bicycle. First, bike straight up the steep hill. Then, bike up the hill again, but this time try to zigzag gently from one side to the other.

Always wear a helmet when riding a bike!

So Simple!

You should have found that it was easier to walk or bike up the hill by taking a zigzag route. This is because you were moving up a shallow slope instead of a steep slope. However, you should have noticed that you had to travel much farther when you zigzagged up the hill.

Amazing Machines

Inclined planes make our lives easier by allowing us to move and lift heavy objects more easily. They let us lift heavy things that would otherwise be impossible to lift straight upward from the ground into vehicles. Inclined planes allow vehicles to be loaded into airplanes and onto ships and trucks. They also help vehicles and trains travel uphill.

What Did You Learn?

Have you tried the simple experiments in this book? What did you learn about inclined planes?

Coal is moved to the top of a huge pile by an inclined plane with a conveyor belt.

The conveyor belt on this inclined plane carries luggage up to the hold of an airliner.

In Big Machines

Inclined planes are simple machines that can be useful on their own. However, we also find them in complicated machines. Some machines with moving parts also use inclined planes. These complex machines include **conveyor belts**, such as the ones that move coal in mines and rock in quarries. They are also used at airports to move luggage.

Can't Live Without Them

People have used inclined planes for thousands of years. They might be simple, but it would be almost impossible for us to live without them. There are probably more of them around than you think. Keep an eye out for inclined planes wherever you go!

Glossary

conveyor belts (kun-VAY-er-BELTZ) Machines that move material by means of a moving belt.

cradles (KRAY-dulz) Frameworks that support things.

force (FORS) A push or a pull.

grade (GRAYD) A measure of the steepness of a slope.

gradient (GRAY-dee-int) A measure of the steepness of a slope.

inclined plane (in-KLYND-PLAYN) A slope used as a simple machine.

levers (LEH-vurs) Rods or bars that move around points called fulcrums.

load (LOHD) The push or pull that an inclined plane overcomes, which may be the weight of an object.

loading ramps (LOH-ding RAMPS) Inclined planes used to move heavy objects into trucks and onto ships.

magnitude (MAG-nih-tood) The measurement of something's strength.

pulleys (PU-leez) Wheels with ropes around them that work as simple machines.

screws (SKROOZ) Simple machines with inclined planes wrapped around cylinders.

vertically (VER-toh-kul-ee) Straight up and down.

wedges (WEJ-ez) Triangular objects used as simple machines.

weight (WAYT) The force of gravity on an object, which pulls the object downward.

wheel and axles (WEEL AND AK-sulz) Simple machines made up of disks with fixed bars running through their centers.

Read More

To learn more about inclined planes, check out these interesting books:

Christiansen, Jennifer. *Get to Know Inclined Planes.* Get to Know Simple Machines. New York: Crabtree Publishing Company, 2009.

Dahl, Michael. *Roll, Slope, and Slide: A Book About Ramps.* Amazing Science: Simple Machines. Mankato, MN: Picture Window Books, 2007.

Gosman, Gillian. *Wheels and Axles in Action.* Simple Machines at Work. New York: PowerKids Press, 2011.

Thales, Sharon. *Inclined Planes to the Rescue.* Simple Machines to the Rescue. Mankato, MN: Capstone Press, 2007.

Yasuda, Anita. *Explore Simple Machines!* Explore Your World. White River Junction, VT: Nomad Press, 2011.

Websites

For web resources related to the subject of this book, go to: www.windmillbooks.com/weblinks and select this book's title.

Index